The Ultimate Love Affair Journal

The Ultimate Love Affair

Affair

~~~

40-Day Companion Journal

April O'Leary

Copyright © 2018 by April O'Leary

Second Printing © 2022

All rights reserved.

Published in the United States by O'Leary Publishing
www.olearypublishing.com

For bulk group pricing please email:
admin@olearypublishing.com

ISBN: 978-1-952491-46-7

Cover Design by Christine Dupre
Photography by Jenna DeSola
Interior Design by Aalisha Mehra
Editing by Joy Xiang

Printed in the United States of America

Also by April O'Leary

Ride the Wave: Journey to Peaceful Living

Focus on You, Your Needs Matter Too!: 6 Simple Lessons to Help You Take Better Care of You

The Networking Revolution: 5 Ways Women Are Changing Their Lives Through Home Business Ownership

The Ultimate Love Affair: Awaken to God's Love Within in Just 40 Days

To you, the reader, who is willing to awaken to God's love again. May this journal help you find what you are looking for!

Table of Contents

Journal Tracker 1

Day 1: What to Give Up... 2

Day 2: Feeling Seen 4

Day 3: Seeing God Rightly 6

Day 4: Focus, Feelings and Faith 8

Day 5: Understanding Self-Love 10

Day 6: Self-Love and Judging Rightly 12

Day 7: Boundaries and Betrayals 14

Day 8: Spending Time Alone 16

Day 9: Overwhelmed by God 18

Day 10: The Power of Asking 20

Day 11: Healing a Hurting Heart 22

Day 12: Knowing Your Truth 24

Day 13: Irrevocable Gifts 26

Day 14: The Answers are Within 28

Day 15: Choosing Truth 30

Day 16: Wait for the Miracle 32

Day 17: Doing the Next Right Thing 34

Day 18: It Starts Inside 36

Day 19: Enduring Hard Things 38

Day 20: Half Measures Availed Us Nothing 40

Day 21: If Nothing Changes... 42

Day 22: When God Ran 44

Day 23: Respecting The Gift 46
Day 24: Knowing Home 48
Day 25: Love Without Fear 50
Day 26: It's Not You 52
Day 27: Choosing Courage 54
Day 28: What If 56
Day 29: It's Not The Thing 60
Day 30: More Questions Than Answers 62
Day 31: Love Above All 64
Day 32: Love and Tolerance 66
Day 33: Choosing Persistence 68
Day 34: Now Go and Remember 70
Day 35: Accepting Reality 72
Day 36: Filling Your God Hole 74
Day 37: Unspeakable Love 76
Day 38: The Love of Money 78
Day 39: Remember Your Chains 80
Day 40: God Is There 82
    Continuing Your Love Affair 84

The Ultimate Love Affair Journal:

Suggestions For Awakening to God's Love Within

The only way we can grow beyond where we currently are is to connect more deeply with God's truth and let go of the bullshit that has been holding us back from hearing God's voice and experiencing His love.

Yes. I just said bullshit.

Since you bought this journal I am certain you are someone who wants to lay the ax to the root and really disconnect from the lies and the negativity that has kept you stuck in patterns that are resurfacing and repeating day in and day out. Right?

Yes. I'll say Amen to that.

Or maybe you are someone who has your shit together, for the most part, but you are feeling tired, worn out and disconnected. You once had a deep connection with God and somewhere along the way you became overly self-sufficient and began running the show, YOUR show, the way you wanted it run. And this way of living has run YOU into the ground.

No shame. That is me too.

I wrote this book and put together this journal as a way to slow down and see how God has used the tragedy in my past for good. Looking in hindsight gives me faith today that if I have weathered all this before, I know that I am more than a conqueror in all things… eventually. Maybe not today. But soon.

This journal is meant to give you a way to dig through some of your interior landscape and see the ways in which God has used your messes to turn your life into a mess-age. Even if you are still in the midst of some craziness you can build your faith simply, day-by-day, through meditating on His word, reciting the daily prayer and spending some time writing through your thoughts and ideas.

My rules for this journal are as follows:

1) You may not judge yourself. Write down whatever you wish and accept it as your truth for right now. No censoring. No trying to sound good on paper.

2) Ask God to speak to your heart as you write. You will be surprised what comes out.

3) Don't worry about grammar, spelling or punctuation. Cross out words, doodle, circle and highlight. Anything goes.

4) Decide right now that you WILL finish this 40-day journey. Put a repeating event on your calendar. Mark the start date and the finish date on the following page. Then be accountable to yourself to finish.

5) Better yet! Recruit some friends to do it with you. You can invite them to get their free copy of The Ultimate Love Affair at www.ultimateaffairbook.com and remind them to also buy the journal. You know people who work with two accountability partners are 87% more likely to stick with it right? That's just simple science. Give yourself the best shot at completing it!

6) When you do work with others you are highly encouraged to practice love and tolerance. Allow people to grow at their own pace and resist the temptation to debate or coerce. Trust that God is working with them too.

I'm so grateful that you have decided to Awaken God's Love Within over these next 40 days. You are going to find a renewed richness to your relationship with God that you have not experienced before. I am praying for you everyday.

May God show Himself mightily to you now.

Love ya!

April

Journal Tracker

My start date is

_____

My finish date is

_____

Check each box below as you finish that day. Yes you can!

Day 1	Day 2	Day 3	Day 4	Day 5	Day 6	Day 7	Day 8	Day 9	Day 10
Day 11	Day 12	Day 13	Day 14	Day 15	Day 16	Day 17	Day 18	Day 19	Day 20
Day 21	Day 22	Day 23	Day 24	Day 25	Day 26	Day 27	Day 28	Day 29	Day 30
Day 31	Day 32	Day 33	Day 34	Day 35	Day 36	Day 37	Day 38	Day 29	Day 40

The Ultimate Love Affair Journal

DAY 1

What to Give Up...

Prayer:

Forgive me for thinking that if it was to be, it's up to me. I humbly show You my Love List, which I am asking for and putting in Your hands. And I'm going to be totally honest and just ask because You said, *Ask and you shall receive, seek and you shall find, knock and it shall be opened.*

I know that I cannot do these things on my own. The list I made is so huge. It feels overwhelming. And that is exactly why I need Your help. Show me how we can be partners and help me focus my time and energy with You on these projects. Give me direction on what I need to cut out of my life to be fully present. I know gifts are freely given, so I believe that You want me to have these things.

I will admit that I am afraid that I am insufficient. I am scared that I am not enough. I know You're not judging me and You know my thoughts already. I think what's most important is that I share them honestly. For too long I've tried to say the *right* things in prayer. I said what I thought You wanted to hear. I was dishonest and sugar-coating my feelings. Pretending. As if You don't know my thoughts already. Who was I fooling? Myself only. I think in part prayer is an admitting to ourselves our feelings and exposing them for what they are. That's self-honesty. Right?

You do care for me. That's so fun and reassuring. Sometimes I feel like I am the one caring for everyone else. And then I wonder who really cares about me? And am I selfish for wanting to be noticed? I'm so glad You do! Thank You for loving me and giving me the power to carry out Your will in the world. What a responsibility and privilege. I will do my best and with Your help WE can.

Scripture:

No, despite all these things, overwhelming victory is ours through Christ, who loved us. Romans 8:37

Ask God right now what He would like to say to you today. Start writing.

DAY 2

Feeling Seen

Prayer:

God, I ask for the courage to face life with complete self-honesty. Knowing that You see me and You understand. Keep me in the palm of Your hand. Let me remember that Your love and acceptance is ever-present. I am not striving to earn it. It is already here in its fullness.

Speak through me and let me see the wonder and beauty You see in me. May I remember when self-doubt creeps in that You are there, and I am not alone. Help me to be more aware when I am looking for acceptance and recognition from others. Release me from that heavy burden.

Help me to walk tall even when others don't understand or approve of what I am doing. Knowing that even Jesus was not welcome in his hometown. Let me accept that even those closest to me might not see the gifts You've given me. And that's ok. I trust You to reveal the truth in time. Thank You for Your patience as I continue to grow. Show me day by day Your love for me. Help me to rest in You.

Scripture:

Before a word is on my tongue
  you, Lord, know it completely.

You hem me in behind and before,
  and you lay your hand upon me.
Such knowledge is too wonderful for me,
  too lofty for me to attain.

Psalm 139: 4-6

Ask God right now what He would like to say to you today. Start writing.

DAY 3

Seeing God Rightly

Prayer:

Forgive me for not seeing You rightly. Forgive me for thinking You are harsh and judgmental. Forgive me for believing You didn't care. I see that I was totally wrong.

Despite my error, thank You for allowing me to re-choose my perceptions of You today. I choose to see how greatly You love me. How much You adore me. How happy You are when I spend time with You. How, like a proud father in the bleachers, You are cheering me on.

Thank You that when I fall You pick me up and reassure me that everything will be alright. You teach me gently and bandage my knee. When I score the game-winning point You are cheering the loudest. You are always proud of me for getting out there and trying. Never judging my attempts to experiment. Never walking away in disgust.

Thank You for allowing me time and space to grow, and thank You that Your patient love never fails. I'm forever grateful for Your love for me...faults and all!

Scripture:

The master said, 'Well done, my good and faithful servant. You have been faithful in handling this small amount, so now I will give you many more responsibilities. Let's celebrate together! Matthew 12:23

Ask God right now what He would like to say to you today. Start writing.

The Ultimate Love Affair Journal

DAY 4

Focus, Feelings and Faith

Prayer:

Today I choose to let go of fear, anxiety, doubt and discouragement. I trust that You have a plan and that all things are working together for my good. I know that sometime in the near future I'll look back at this moment and say, "Wow if it weren't for that happening then this wouldn't have happened!"

So while I'm in the midst of the storm, even then shall I praise You. Knowing that You are Lord of it all. You see things I can't see right now and I will hang onto the promises that You love me, You see me and You understand my needs in ways I don't.

I am excited to see how this will work knowing that all glory will go to You because I could never take credit for pulling this off myself. I will go where You lead with the confidence that You are working out all the details. Amen.

Scripture:

And we know that God causes everything to work together for the good of those who love God and are called according to his purpose for them. Romans 8:28

Ask God right now what He would like to say to you today. Start writing.

DAY 5

Understanding Self-Love

Prayer:

Can I really love myself as much as I love others without being selfish? Can it be that I had it all wrong? Thank You for showing me ways in which I have misunderstood my position as a treasured and loved Child of God.

Give me the confidence to take better care of myself so I can be a better example of Your love in the world. Free me from resentment, frustration, guilt, depression and anger. Let me see those feelings as red flags that I have done too much for others and not enough for myself.

Today, I pray that You would show me how to let go of fear in loving myself as You love me. Help me to see where I need to set healthier boundaries with those who are draining my time and energy. Help me to look to You first for love. Even today, I will heighten my awareness of how much You love me.

Thank You Jesus for modeling the way to connect with the Father, fill myself and then serve others. I will follow You. Amen.

Scripture:

And you must love the Lord your God with all your heart, all your soul, all your mind, and all your strength.' The second is equally important: 'Love your neighbor as yourself.' No other commandment is greater than these." Mark 12:30-31

Ask God right now what He would like to say to you today. Start writing.

DAY 6

Self-Love and Judging Rightly

Prayer:

For so long I have not wanted to acknowledge that evil exists in the world. I thought that my love could save even the darkest of hearts. But today I see my own limitations and know that to love myself means giving up the idea that I can help and should help everyone.

You have the power to change the heart of any man or woman who is open to change. Help me to see who is truly open to receiving Your love and to discern who is not. Let me not waste time with people who don't want help.

Let me be highly protective of my time and energy, and use it in a way that is productive and healthy both for me and those who You might put in my path who I can touch with Your hand. I will do my best to rid my life of toxic people who drain my time and energy.

Give me strength and courage to do so. I am so grateful for Your direction to judge people by their fruits. Thank You for showing me the way. Amen.

Scripture:

But the Holy Spirit produces this kind of fruit in our lives: love, joy, peace, patience, kindness, goodness, faithfulness, gentleness and self-control. There is no law against these things! Galatians 5:22-23.

Ask God right now what He would like to say to you today. Start writing.

DAY 7

Boundaries and Betrayals

Prayer:

Who can understand the power of Your love? Even You had to go through the pain of betrayal. How can it be? Help me to believe the best in others and also to believe the facts when someone shows me who they really are.

Give me the courage to let go. Bring strong people into my life who can speak words of comfort and wisdom to me and give me the heart to believe them. I don't want to live in ignorance. I want to be of maximum service to You.

May I learn what I need to learn from toxic relationships, if and when they creep into my life, and help me to recognize that it is not of my doing and that You have the power to deal with their heart. My job is to trust You and set healthier tighter boundaries with that person. Give me the strength to move on and the grace to forgive myself.

Thank You for showing me that, however painful it is. Betrayal is sometimes a part of life. I will not lose faith during these times but will lean into Your love. Thank You that You will never leave me or forsake me. Amen.

Scripture:

Let your conduct be without covetousness; be content with such things as you have. For He Himself has said, "I will never leave you nor forsake you." Hebrews 13:5

Ask God right now what He would like to say to you today. Start writing.

DAY 8

Spending Time Alone

Prayer:

Today, I pray that You would help me to slow down and accept my need for rest and refueling. Let me not think of it as selfish but as necessary. Help me to let go of the unhealthy guilt that would prevent me from taking time away from the demands of life to reconnect with You. Help me to honor my feelings as a wise compass.

Speak to me in our private times together. Let me feel Your love from the inside and pour it outwards to others from the abundance that I have received. I know that all good things come from above and You will lead me beside the still waters and restore my soul. Let me rest today knowing that You care for me.

Scripture:

The Lord is my shepherd;

I shall not want.

He makes me to lie down in green pastures;

He leads me beside the still waters.

He restores my soul;

He leads me in the paths of righteousness

For His name's sake.

Psalm 23:1-3

Ask God right now what He would like to say to you today. Start writing.

DAY 9

Overwhelmed by God

Prayer:

Forgive me for not trusting You in everything. I believe that all things will work together for my good even though I don't see how it could right now. Today I make a decision to turn my will and my life over to Your care because You care for me. I admit that I don't see the whole picture, and that is why I am excited to see how You will work out the details of this situation in ways I could have never predicted or planned.

Thank You that I don't have to walk through this life alone, and that I don't have to have all the answers. Instead of self-sufficiency, I will rely on You. Thank you for caring! Thank You for loving! Thank You for calling me to greatness despite my human frailties. May any success I have point back to You. Amen.

Scripture:

Casting all your anxieties on him, because he cares for you. 1 Peter 5:7

Ask God right now what He would like to say to you today. Start writing.

DAY 10

The Power of Asking

Prayer:

Is it really so easy? Forgive me for making life harder than it needs to be through relying on my own strength, smarts and attitude of self-sufficiency. Forgive me for thinking You were too busy to help and that I would be bothering You with my problems. Today, I ask that You reveal Your will to me and give me the power to carry it out.

Help me to remember that You are always with me and want to help me just as a concerned parent wants to help their child. Thank You for being interested in the details of my life. I am so grateful I don't have to walk this path alone. For You are with me. You uphold me with Your right hand, and You keep me safe in the shadow of Your wings. What do I have to fear with You by my side!

I will look for answers today in the people I meet, the places I go, the conversations I have and the books I read. I will be open to seeing You revealed right in front of me. I'm excited to see what this day will bring. Thank You for all You are to me. I am falling in love with You again.

Scripture:

Be anxious for nothing, but in everything by prayer and supplication with thanksgiving let your requests be made known to God. Philippians 4:6

Ask God right now what He would like to say to you today. Start writing.

DAY 11

Healing a Hurting Heart

Prayer:

I wish I could put together the right words and make it sound good, but I'm tired of hiding. You know my heart and my thoughts anyway, so I may as well tell You the truth. I have made mistakes I'd prefer not to admit to You or to anyone. I am embarrassed and have held myself at a distance from You trying to pretend everything was okay when it wasn't. But I know better now.

Today, I choose courage over pride. I am grateful that I have the ability to ask forgiveness and do better next time. I know I am a work in progress. You know that too. You made me, with all my gifts and all my humanness, and You love me fully today exactly as I am. There is nothing I can do to earn more of Your love. I accept it with a humble heart and say thank You.

May I always remain open and honest with You and myself. I know it is this foundation that will cause my life to be solid and secure in You. I ask this all in Your name.

Scripture:

For everything that is hidden will eventually be brought into the open, and every secret will be brought to light. Mark 4:22

Ask God right now what He would like to say to you today. Start writing.

DAY 12

Knowing Your Truth

Prayer:

God, I know You are everywhere at all times. You speak to all people, and there is no barrier to the heart. The words may be different, but the Holy Spirit is One and the same. Your eyes see more deeply, and You said we will know our brothers and sisters of faith by their fruits.

Help me see ways I have been judgmental and arrogant. Help me to walk humbly, do justly and to love mercy. Give me faith to let the real me shine brighter than the false me I safely show others. Let alignment with Your will be my utmost goal.

Help me to boldly step under the flow of Your outpouring love and gifts and share them in full strength to the world. May I be of maximum service to You. For I know I am fearfully and wonderfully made.

Scripture:

I will praise You, for I am fearfully and wonderfully made;

Marvelous are Your works,

And that my soul knows very well.

Psalm 139:14

NOTE: To view a very powerful TedX talk called "Have you met your soulmate?" featuring Ashley Clift-Jennings, which discusses transgender issues, please visit www.aprilolerary.com/ultimateresources.

Ask God right now what He would like to say to you today. Start writing.

DAY 13

Irrevocable Gifts

Prayer:

It's been so long since I have considered my own feelings of unfulfillment. I have tried to be content with what I have, and now I can see that it is not that I am ungrateful, I am living outside of my gifts and calling. You have allowed a lingering discontent to sit on my shoulder to prod me back to what You know I would be gifted doing. Help me to have faith to take even the smallest step in that direction.

Reveal to me ways that I can start to reawaken my desire to live in alignment with the gifts You have so generously given me. Forgive me for not trusting that they were valuable and for trying to do things my own way. Open doors that only You can open. Bring people my way who will help give me clear direction.

Please give me a peace that passes all understanding as I get honest with myself and live closer to You. May the way come smoothly. Your yoke is easy, and Your burden is light. I know You will give me rest. In my heart. In my body. In my mind. In my spirit. You know the way. I will follow.

Scripture:

Eye has not seen, nor ear heard,

Nor have entered into the heart of man

The things which God has prepared for those who love Him.

1 Corinthians 2:9

Ask God right now what He would like to say to you today. Start writing.

DAY 14

The Answers are Within

Prayer:

What marvelous gifts You have given me. That I may use them to my highest capability is my heart's cry. I know that I am fearfully and wonderfully made, and yet sometimes I don't understand myself all that well. Reveal to me the ways that I can better understand and maximize the gifts You have given me. I am willing to dig and see what motivates me and then use that self-knowledge to make this world a better place.

Thank You for making me so unique and help me to trust my intuition and the guidance of the Holy Spirit over the opinions and approval of others. I am grateful that You love me just as I am. I will seek Your thoughts on a matter first. And I know out of the good treasure of my heart, I will bring forth good things. Onward and Upward. Together we will climb.

Scripture:

For My thoughts are not Your thoughts,

Nor are Your ways My ways," says the Lord.

"For as the heavens are higher than the earth,

So are My ways higher than your ways,

And My thoughts than your thoughts."

Isaiah 55:8-9

Ask God right now what He would like to say to you today. Start writing.

DAY 15

Choosing Truth

Prayer:

I'm having a hard time believing that You don't judge me. But You said You don't, so I'll take You at Your Word. Help me to not judge others. Help me to not judge situations and jump to conclusions. Help me to slow down and acknowledge that I only know a very little about anyone or any situation I encounter. Help me to see life as a moment-by-moment unfolding of perfection. That You are orchestrating the events of my life to help me awaken to peace and trust You more.

Help me also to accept responsibility for my emotions and when they are rough, let me go to prayer and ask for Your eyes. I want to see people as You see them. Loved. And maybe they are just living in unawareness of You. No wonder so many people are tired and frustrated and angry and hopeless. Let me be the light in their day. The smile that lets them know there is more to life than just the simple tasks that make up our days. You were certain of Yourself. You knew where You came from and where You were going. May I also have that same confidence to walk through life not needing others to conform to my will, but that I would be willing to conform to Yours.

I want to be free from allowing the external situations of my life to control my mood. That is true freedom, and I can see that it is possible if I'm willing to practice. Thank You for being patient with me. I choose peace. I choose truth. I choose freedom.

Scripture:

Where the Spirit of the Lord is, there is freedom. 2 Corinthians 3:17

Ask God right now what He would like to say to you today. Start writing.

DAY 16

Wait for the Miracle

Prayer:

I am tired of relying on my own strength. I have been self-sufficient for so long. I am ready to step out in faith and walk into the wilderness where I have to rely on You to provide for me. Help me to trust that You care for me. That You won't let me faint. That if You provide for the birds of the air, You will provide for me too.

I am willing to do my part. I will learn what I need to learn, and seek out a mentor who can help me and take the necessary steps in this physical realm to support the spiritual breakthrough I am seeking. But I know that it is not my doing that will cause this miracle. It's my investment of time meditating on Your Word, my commitment to prayer and my desire to seek first Your kingdom, that matters most. I know only then will all these things will be added unto me. Why? Because you promised it.

I am so grateful that I am not alone. Give me the stamina and persistence to stay the course and not walk home before the miracle happens.

Scripture:

But those who trust in the LORD will find new strength. They will soar high on wings like eagles. They will run and not grow weary. They will walk and not faint. Isaiah 40:31

Ask God right now what He would like to say to you today. Start writing.

DAY 17

Doing the Next Right Thing

Prayer:

What power You have given me between my ears. I confess I have not managed my thought life to the best of my ability. In fact, up until now I was largely unaware of how crazy I have allowed myself to think at times. I'm grateful that Your Word can be a light unto my path. That it can light up the thoughts and beliefs that don't align with who You say that I am and that I can choose to shift my focus and thinking to the Truth of being a worthy and loved child of God.

Help me today to be aware of when I allow my thinking to slip into negativity and untruth. Help me to catch it and replace the thought with Your thoughts. Let me see every time I do that, a seed being planted in my heart that will yield a harvest of a beautiful and fruitful life that is pleasing to You. May I be of maximum service in all that I do, starting with my commitment to a right thought life. I know with Your help, I can do it. One day at a time.

Scripture:

But the Advocate, the Holy Spirit, whom the Father will send in My Name, will teach you all things and will remind you of everything I have said to you. Peace I leave with you; My peace I give you. I do not give to you as the world gives. Do not let your hearts be troubled and do not be afraid. John 14: 26-27

Ask God right now what He would like to say to you today. Start writing.

DAY 18

It Starts Inside

Prayer:

I am starting to make the connection between my inner world and my outer experiences. It's freeing to know that I can stop trying to control and fix everything outside of me and start with the awareness that it is the matters of the heart and mind where I can make the biggest change. Help me to be more aware of my negative thinking.

Help me to see it for what it is, not sinful, just undisciplined. Help me to detach from those thoughts that don't serve the higher purpose You have called me to, and let them leave my mind as quickly as they came. I am willing to be open to practicing meditation and becoming more aware of my thoughts. I will practice exercising self-discipline in my mind and heart every day. I will have faith that as I do this my outer world will change too.

Thank You for sharing the secrets of the kingdom with me today. Your ways are higher than mine and now I understand that I have been focusing too long on the outside and will focus more on my inner reality. Thank You for Your patience and love for me as I continue to grow.

Scripture:

But they delight in the law of the Lord,
  meditating on it day and night.
They are like trees planted along the riverbank,
  bearing fruit each season.
Their leaves never wither,
  and they prosper in all they do.

Psalm 1: 2-3

Ask God right now what He would like to say to you today. Start writing.

DAY 19

Enduring Hard Things

Prayer:

Thank You God for Your patience with me. Even when I have been a complainer. An ungrateful child and a doubter. Forgive me for not trusting the path that You have laid before me. Forgive me for assuming my life was supposed to be trial-free. Forgive me for thinking, "WHY ME?"

Thank You for reminding me in Philippians, "but this one thing I do, forgetting those things which are behind, and reaching forth unto those things which are before, I press toward the mark for the prize of the high calling of God in Christ Jesus."

Let me forget what is behind me. I will not ruminate on it, rehash it, question it or despise it. I will learn from it and when I can't get beyond it alone, I will seek the help of my pastor or another professional. I choose to see Your grace and mercy in all of it. I will allow my trials to draw me closer to You. In the midst of them, I will praise You because I know the end of a thing is better than the beginning.

I know You are working all things together for good for me and I choose to trust You today in the mess knowing that it will someday be my mess-age to help draw others to You. Your ways are higher. And I'm so glad about that.

Scripture:

Better is the end of a thing than the beginning thereof: and the patient in spirit is better than the proud in spirit. Ecclesiastes 7:8

Ask God right now what He would like to say to you today. Start writing.

DAY 20

Half Measures Availed Us Nothing

Prayer:

I know I've held back my full trust and full commitment. I haven't wanted to fully let go and follow Your plan. Maybe I thought that seemed irresponsible.? Maybe I didn't understand what that looked like? Maybe I have been so used to doing it my way that consulting with You wasn't even a part of my thought process? For that I am sorry. Please forgive me.

I don't want to circle the same mountain anymore. I don't want to get stuck in excuses and blaming others. I accept full responsibility for my life and for the results I've had up to this point. I know that if I continue to do the same thing, I cannot expect anything different than what I currently have. And I want more peace. I want rest for my soul. I want to learn from You.

Help me to catch myself when I am tempted to fall back into self-sufficiency mode. Let me crack open the door of my heart to allow You in. Be my coach, my confidant and my co-counsel. Let me clearly hear Your voice and help me to be willing to take action even on ideas that might seem impossible. I'm willing to pick up my mat and walk. I know when I follow You, You will give me the desires of my heart. I'm all in.

Scripture:

Take delight in the Lord, and He will give you the desires of your heart.

Psalm 37:4

Ask God right now what He would like to say to you today. Start writing.

DAY 21

If Nothing Changes...

Prayer:

Changing others is what I have been overly focused on for too long. I see now that it's my ego that wants them to be wrong and I want to be right. Forgive me for thinking I know what is better for someone else than they do. Forgive me for blocking Your ability to reach them by being overly-concerned, overly-involved and overly-worried. You see their hearts and I release them to You.

Even though it's hard and my heart hurts over this reality, I know that I need to focus on what I can change. And that is me. Give me the strength to accept this reality. Give me the peace to move forward into Your will for me today. Let me not circle the same mountain of discontent thinking it will change if I don't change.

Help me to stop waiting for others to do something, and let me see the truth of the matter. If there is something I don't see clearly, reveal it to me through prayer and through the conversations of trusted others who have my best interest at heart. Give me the courage to allow them to speak into my life.

I want to be a vessel You can use and not be dragged down by the cares and worries of this world. I see now that my life is comprised of everything I have chosen up to this point, and I am willing to choose more wisely who I spend my time, my money, my energy with. Thank You for waiting for me patiently. I'm so grateful.

Scripture:

The Lord isn't really being slow about His promise, as some people think. No, He is being patient for your sake. He does not want anyone to be destroyed, but wants everyone to repent. 2 Peter 3:9

Ask God right now what He would like to say to you today. Start writing.

DAY 22

When God Ran

Prayer:

I can't understand Your love for me. My human brain is incapable of grasping the depth and breadth of it. Why me? What did I do to deserve it? Nothing. That's what. You created me in Your image and You said "It is good." Thank You for seeing the good in me even when I falter. Thank You for believing the best in me when I stray. Thank You for watching out the window for my return.

Help me to guard my heart against resentfulness that can creep in when I mistakenly believe I am doing something to earn Your approval. Help me to see it is Your grace that is sufficient for me. Also help me to stay on the path and not manipulate Your love. It is tempting to want to ask for the inheritance and then squander it knowing You'll take me back in.

May my heart remain pure, and may I take delight in all that You have promised me is mine. It is not "out there" and You are not withholding anything from me. Let me ask for those things I need knowing that You will give them to me, not because I am deserving, but because You love me and it delights You to give me good things. Thank You for releasing me to freedom in Your love.

Scripture:

The Lord is compassionate and merciful, slow to get angry and filled with unfailing love. He will not constantly accuse us, nor remain angry forever. He does not punish us for all our sins; He does not deal harshly with us, as we deserve. For His unfailing love toward those who fear Him is as great as the height of the heavens above the earth. He has removed our sins as far from us as the east is from the west. The Lord is like a father to His children, tender and compassionate to those who fear Him.

Psalm 103:8-13

Ask God right now what He would like to say to you today. Start writing.

DAY 23

Respecting The Gift

Prayer:

Thank You so much for the moments of clarity I have already had in my life. For the times You have protected me when I didn't know it and for Your hand that was on me and patiently waiting for me even when I was completely unaware that my path was destroying my life. I was to remove the blocks and distance I have unknowingly placed between us. I want to see them for what they are. A distraction. A destruction. And also a gift.

I know that the crises in my life can bring about good. I don't want to wait for them though. I want to see them before I crash and burn. Help me to listen to the promptings of the Spirit when I get off course and walk away from You. Help me to turn my feet and return back home. More than that, help me to remain home with an attitude of gratefulness for Your compassion and love.

Help me to see all the ways that You have been so good to me and to respect the gift, holding onto it with my life. Forgive me for the ways in which I have not respected all You have given to me. Let me love You above all else in word, in deed and with a pure heart.

Scripture:

So humble yourselves under the mighty power of God, and at the right time he will lift you up in honor. Give all your worries and cares to God, for he cares about you. Stay alert! Watch out for your great enemy, the devil. He prowls around like a roaring lion, looking for someone to devour. Stand firm against him, and be strong in your faith. 1 Peter 5:6-9

Ask God right now what He would like to say to you today. Start writing.

DAY 24

Knowing Home

Prayer:

The power of Your love—who can understand it? The unexpected nature of Your time on earth. Days spent healing those who were sick in body and spirit, pouring out the Father's love into the hearts of those who were hurting and never taking credit for it. May I be able to love like that. With no strings attached. With no agenda. From a connection to the power source, which is You.

When I ask for Your love and power to flow through me, help me to remember that is not me doing the works but You. It's hard to love as You did. Unselfishly. Forgive me for wanting something back or giving expecting to receive. That is not how You showed me.

Help me to keep my focus on You and trust that You will take care of my every need. Help me to humbly receive love when it is offered and see it as an expression of Your love towards me. Thank You for showing me how to love through Your perfect example may I grow more like You each day. Give me an opportunity today to show Your love to someone who needs it.

Scripture:

...and hope does not disappoint, because the love of God has been poured out within our hearts through the Holy Spirit who was given to us Romans 5:5

Ask God right now what He would like to say to you today. Start writing.

DAY 25

Love Without Fear

Prayer:

Fearless in life and fearless in death. That is how I want to live. To recklessly abandon myself and accept Your love is the most powerful thing I can do in this lifetime. Setting aside every weight. The weight of self-criticism. The weight of doubting. The weight of lack. And connecting fully to my worth which comes from You.

I know it is the Spirit which gives life to the body. And the same Spirit that resided in Jesus, is living in me now. Not a lesser degree, not a lower quality, the same Spirit! It is the fear I allow to reside in my heart and mind that blocks the power of Your Love from flowing through me purely.

May I recognized fear for the liar it is and cast out those characters that want me to believe I am not enough. I AM enough. I believe You have called me to be Your light in the world. May I shine as brightly as possible, allowing Your Love to power my body and draw people to You, in life and in death. I will not fear.

Scripture:

And now these three remain: faith, hope and love. But the greatest of these is love. I Corinthians 13:13

Ask God right now what He would like to say to you today. Start writing.

DAY 26

It's Not You

Prayer:

Forgive me for thinking anything I do is a success because of me. Forgive me to allowing myself to think that the ideas I've had are mine. Thank You for giving them to me. Thank You for speaking to me in ways that I can hear and understand. Thank You for the willingness to carry out Your work in the world. Even in the small ways I do.

I am grateful to be a part of Your Missions Team. It must have been hard to not allow pride to take over Your ministry, Jesus. After all, I'm sure people were looking to You as their human Savior, the endpoint to the miracles You so powerfully executed. It would have been easy to use that human power and authority to manipulate people and elevate Your own status. Yet You never did that. You walked humbly. You resisted temptation.

You always kept a mindful watch on Your heart and committed to showing up early in the morning for prayer and reconnection with Your source. The Father. May I follow Your example. May I always remember that any small or great success I experience in this lifetime is Your work being done through me. All credit is Yours. I am here. Willing. Use me. Choose me.

Scripture:

Oh, how great are God's riches and wisdom and knowledge! How impossible it is for us to understand his decisions and his ways! Romans 11:33

Ask God right now what He would like to say to you today. Start writing.

DAY 27

Choosing Courage

Prayer:

How often I have allowed pride to steer me off course. Away from the love You have poured out on me. I have been afraid to make changes in areas I know clearly are not working. Forgive me for not trusting You. Help me to see what I can do today to choose courage. I feel scared. Alone. Sometimes even just a little unwilling to make a change.

Forgive me for not believing You have a better life for me. Forgive me for being apathetic and accepting of people and situations that are not serving You or me. Forgive me for not showing up in this life as a conduit of Your love at all times. Forgive me for choosing fear and pride over courage.

I ask today that You give me the willingness to change. I ask that You give me the right words to say. I ask that You send the right people along my path who can help me. I ask that when the opportunity arises that despite anxiety or anger or hate, I would choose courage. I pray that in that moment I will trust You and be sensitive to the inner voice that is directing me.

Thank You for all the hurdles in my life right now that are giving me the opportunity to learn and grow up. I don't want to circle this mountain for another decade. I don't even want to circle it for one more day. Help me to correct course. Today.

Scripture:

So be strong and courageous! Do not be afraid and do not panic before them. For the Lord your God will personally go ahead of you. He will neither fail you nor abandon you. Deuteronomy 31:6

Ask God right now what He would like to say to you today. Start writing.

DAY 28

What If...

What If (a poem based on Psalm 139) by April O'Leary

What if You knew everything about me and loved me anyways?

The loving part of me and the hateful part of me.

The generous part of me and the prideful part of me.

The part of me that wants to be seen and that part of me that wants to stay hidden from you.

What if....

What if You knew when I sat down and when I stood up?

You see my fits of anger and my gentle hand.

You see my smile in delight and my tears that fall softly with hurt.

You see. And you smile when I smile, cry when I cry and hurt when I hurt.

What if.....

What if you knew what I was going to say even before I spoke a word?

You laugh at my crooked jokes and cringe at my foul language.

You nod at a word spoken in timely fashion and give me words when I don't know what to say.

You know me better than I know myself. And still You love me faults and all.

What if...

What if You place Your hand of blessing on my head?

You have prepared my path and You also respect my will to choose it.

You work things out for me even when I choose the wrong thing.

You know I am growing and You are ever patient with me. Not expecting perfection.

What if...

What if I have it all wrong?

What if I could stop striving?

What if I could simply rest in You?

What if I asked and knew that You could and would help if You were sought?

What if....

I want to believe the What if.

Help me see the What if.

I choose to live the What If.

What if....

Prayer:

What if everything You said about me were true? That You care so deeply. That You love so richly. That You want nothing more than that I feel Your love being shed abroad in my heart at every moment. Perfect love casts out all fear. What if I could live a fearless life? What would I do that I am not doing now? How would I stand taller? Smile more? Laugh with reckless abandon? Could I smile at the future?

All these things I desire so deeply and all these things are mine if I remove the doubt and believe the truth of who You are and then the truth of who I am in You. Let me be all that You have created me to be. Powerful. Happy. Generous. Loved. Seen. May I rely on You for my identity and not on what others have told me in the past. May I see myself as You see me. Thank You for making me wonderful. May I believe that today. I am wonderful. Who would have thought?

Scripture:

Thank you for making me so wonderfully complex!

Your workmanship is marvelous—how well I know it.

Psalm 139:14

Ask God right now what He would like to say to you today. Start writing.

DAY 29

It's Not The Thing

Prayer:

Aiming for understanding. Looking inside not outside of me for peace. I understand that conceptually. Seems easy enough. But I often feel trapped by my circumstances. How can I NOT look at them? I pray that You would help me to see where I am not accepting life on life's terms. I pray that I would be able to let go of control even if it's just so that I have the opportunity to practice trusting You more.

Help me see that I am not a slave to the externals. They are just a roadmap to my heart. Revealing to me the lessons I need to learn today. Do I need more patience? Then I thank You for a long line at the grocery checkout.

In all things, I will look for the lesson. I will soften my heart and see that everything is exactly as it needs to be in this moment. To change anything, I only need to look within and seek Your help and guidance. I will.

Scripture:

I pray that the eyes of your heart may be enlightened, so that you will know what is the hope of His calling, what are the riches of the glory of His inheritance in the saints. Ephesians 1:18

Ask God right now what He would like to say to you today. Start writing.

DAY 30

More Questions Than Answers

Prayer:

Today, help me to stop striving. Eliminate confusion, and help me to trust in the future You have for me. Let me see that it is full of hope. I know I will find You. You promised me that. I will look for You in the eyes of another. In the books that I read. In my Facebook newsfeed. You're out there speaking through people. You want me to find You.

May my heart be willing and open. May it delight in a timely word. May I connect the dots of my life in a way that is meaningful and helpful. May I stop swimming and striving and believe You are just one word away. I will be still and know that You are God.

Scripture:

Even though I walk through the valley of the shadow of death, I fear no evil, for You are with me;

Psalm 23:4

Ask God right now what He would like to say to you today. Start writing.

DAY 31

Love Above All

Prayer:

God, forgive me for majoring on the minors. Forgive me for getting into debates and arguments of doctrines and making my "rightness" more important than showing Your love. Love is my highest calling.

Let me remember that when my heart is racing and I want to get in a last point. Let me remember love when I am feeling threatened and insecure. Let me see that for what it is. My ego, trying to run the show. Help me to surrender to Love.

Help me to see people with Your Eyes. Help me to step out of the way and lower my resistance so they can also lower theirs. I trust that You speak to everyone, and I choose to love. Above All. Let me show Your love.

Let me be patient and kind. Help me to see that no one person holds all the truth, and I only know a small bit. I know but a drop in the ocean of Your wisdom. Help me to let go of my need to be right and choose the softer way. Love. In all things. Love.

Scripture:

If I have the gift of prophecy and can fathom all mysteries and all knowledge, and if I have a faith that can move mountains, but do not have love, I am nothing. 1 Corinthians 13:2

Ask God right now what He would like to say to you today. Start writing.

DAY 32

Love and Tolerance

Prayer:

Forgive me God for being so quick to judge, not just in my heart but in my words and attitudes. What a prideful person I can be! Help me to love those who love You and are trying their best to impact the world.

Help me to allow people the space to exhibit their faith in the way that seems right to them without criticizing or correcting. You speak to the hearts of everyone, and You can use anything and anyone as a way to get Your message to those who are open and seeking. Let me not think that my way is the only way. Remind me that I only know a little bit and what I do know is that Love is always the way.

Thank You for showing me my own hypocrisy and help me to recognize it more quickly next time. Soften my heart toward all of Your children, and let me be one who is willing to see that there is room for everyone to play in the sandbox together.

Scripture:

Make every effort to keep yourselves united in the Spirit, binding yourselves together with peace. Ephesians 4:3

Ask God right now what He would like to say to you today. Start writing.

DAY 33

Choosing Persistence

Prayer:

Thank You that You are a just God and that You actually care about me. Forgive me for being to weak in my requests. For assuming You didn't want me to have the desires of my heart. Forgive me for giving up too soon. I am making a decision today to believe that You want me to have the desires of my heart. You want to make my dreams come true. Nothing would make You happier than to see me thriving in the gifts You have given me.

I ask You today that You bring people along my path who can help me. That You organize the details of my life so that magical things can happen to bring about the desires I have for success and impact. Forgive me for the times I have cut You out of the equation and tried to do it on my own. I need You as my partner.

I am willing to take the actions and I ask that You amplify my actions in such a way that they have maximum results. So that when I see the gifts and the glory unfolding in such a magnificent way, I will know without a doubt, that it is not because I am wise, or smart or gifted, I am just persistent and have put my trust in You. You parted the sea. I took a step to walk through it. Thank You for making a way, when I didn't see how it would happen. You are amazing! I am so grateful. I love You.

Scripture:

Let us therefore come boldly to the throne of grace, that we may obtain mercy and find grace to help in time of need. Hebrews 4:16

Ask God right now what He would like to say to you today. Start writing.

DAY 34

Now Go and Remember

Prayer:

This is the day that the Lord has made, I will rejoice and be glad in it. You know my coming and my going. You know when I sit and when I rise. You are with me day and night. You see me. You have a plan for me and that plan is to share Your love and kindness with others and to walk by faith and not by sight.

Forgive me for the times I have been impulsive and did not seek Your guidance before making a decision and despite this, You entered in and redeemed my hastiness and made it all turn out for the good. Forgive me for the times when I have feared making a decision.

Help me to trust that You will support the details of my life that I decide on based on seeking Your guidance. There is no where I can go that You won't be there. Let me feel safe enough to take action where I have been stuck in inaction.

Today I will make a decision to make a decision. I will rely on the promise You made that when I commit my actions to You my plans WILL succeed. Thank You for trusting me to decide and for giving me free will to work out the details, knowing that there is nothing I can do that will separate me from Your love. Let's rock!

Scripture:

We can make our plans, but the Lord determines our steps.

Proverbs 16:9

Ask God right now what He would like to say to you today. Start writing.

DAY 35

Accepting Reality

Prayer:

God, forgive me for the times that I've fought the realities of life that I didn't want to accept as being exactly the way they were supposed to be. Forgive me for blaming You or myself. Help me to see this world as transient and fleeting and help me to see that there is a purpose for everything.

I can learn in all situations and I know that You have planned my days perfectly. I will accept responsibility for the times I mess up. I will continue to change what I know can be changed. I pray for the wisdom to know the difference. I pray for the peace to accept the season of my life as they come and go. I trust You.

Thank You for the gift of serenity and peace of mind. May I sense when it is elusive and see where I can accept Your Will in that moment. Release me from judging others when they are going through difficult times. May I be a supporter and a friend above all. May I always walk in Your Love and may I have a kind word and a helping hand when others need serenity too.

Scripture:

Finally, all of you should be of one mind. Sympathize with each other. Love each other as brothers and sisters. Be tenderhearted, and keep a humble attitude. 1 Peter 3: 8-9

Ask God right now what He would like to say to you today. Start writing.

DAY 36

Filling Your God Hole

Prayer:

God, forgive me for the times I've been an A-hole, because I haven't sought You and filled my God-hole. Forgive me for trying to cope with life in unhealthy ways, and help me to see that only You can fill that void in my heart. I know it sounds so trite to me at times. But it's true.

You are hiding in plain sight. You are not trying to make it difficult to find You. May I look in the eyes of another and see you today. May I see You in the stars. May I feel You in the hand of another. May I sense Your presence in conversations I have. May I see coincidences as Your way of remaining anonymous.

Help me to remove the blocks that I've created in my mind by believing You need me to do or be something to find You. Help me to rest in the fact that You never left. You are as close now as You ever were. Thank You that nothing can separate me from Your love.

Scripture:

For I am convinced that neither death nor life, neither angels nor demons, neither the present nor the future, nor any powers, neither height nor depth, nor anything else in all creation, will be able to separate us from the love of God that is in Christ Jesus our Lord. Romans 8: 38-39

Ask God right now what He would like to say to you today. Start writing.

DAY 37

Unspeakable Love

Prayer:

I can't understand Your love. How would You be willing to lose your Only Son to give life to me? It doesn't make sense. Yet, I hear Manny and see the faces of the 28 kids who were rescued out of sex trafficking in an effort to find his son, and I can feel the joy and the pain residing in unison. The lives that were freed because of the loss of one. The smiles on their faces not knowing that the one they came for was not among them.

How great is the love You have for me? May this light You have put in my heart shine on others. May it light up the darkness. May Your power make it possible for me to get knocked down and not destroyed. Help me to stand. Help me to get better and not bitter when injustices come. Help me to see that there is a purpose much greater than my human understanding.

May I be more like You. Willing to sacrifice what I have, even what is most precious to me, in order to spread Your freedom and love into a darkened world. May I truly mean that. It's hard to say even now. I don't want to suffer losses. Help me be willing to be willing. Help me. Mould me.

Use me as Your voice for the helpless, Your hands for healing the hurting, Your resources to fund Your work in the world. Let me not sit back and wait for someone else to do it. Give me opportunities to say YES and serve life in a bigger way. I will say YES. Help me to be willing.

Scripture:

We know what real love is because Jesus gave up his life for us. So we also ought to give up our lives for our brothers and sisters. 1 John 3:16

Ask God right now what He would like to say to you today. Start writing.

DAY 38

The Love of Money

Prayer:

What joy it would give me to be able to pay it forward in increasingly bigger and bigger ways. Help me to see more efficient and effective ways to make money. Help me to plug into the right ideas, the right systems and the right relationships to make that happen. Help me to know that You want everything my hand to touch to prosper and believe that as I serve others at higher and higher levels the money will come. I will be a trusted steward and distributor of it to further Your work in the world.

Forgive me for the ways I have squandered what You have given me in the past. Forgive me for acting like a spoiled child. Forgive me for not gaining the knowledge I have needed to be successful and for doubting that You wanted me to live a wealthy life. I know that with the gifts You have given me and the Spirit working in and through me all things are possible. I believe. I will seek opportunities. I ask and I receive.

Thank You for taking care of Me, Your child, in such abundant ways. I know it brings You joy. And it brings me joy too. I will guard my heart from greed and use what You give me generously and wisely. Amen.

Scripture:

The Lord your God will then make you successful in everything you do. Deuteronomy 30:9

Ask God right now what He would like to say to you today. Start writing.

DAY 39

Remember Your Chains

Prayer:

Thank You for another day. I want to hear You say, "Well done good and faithful servant." And I'm willing to change what needs to be changed. It's just that sometimes I don't see it. Let me see with clarity. I ask You to show me patterns that I've had for years that have not served You or me.

Help me to see the mountain I keep circling and have the courage to change. Let me humbly be open to the feedback of others who have my best interest at heart. Let me receive suggestions with an ear to listen to the Holy Spirit and the conviction it might bring. Give me the courage to change.

Release me from the prison of judging and help me to see others as fellow journeymen looking for answers on their own path back to You. Let me love them and extend compassion.

Thank You for Your long-suffering and protection, even when I was unaware and not seeking You. I am forever grateful to have the opportunity to live out Your mission for me in this world. May I rise powerfully to the great calling You have for me. Amen.

Scripture:

Do not remember the former things,
Nor consider the things of old.
Behold, I will do a new thing,
Now it shall spring forth;
Shall you not know it?
I will even make a road in the wilderness
And rivers in the desert.
Isaiah 43: 18-19

Ask God right now what He would like to say to you today. Start writing.

DAY 40

God Is There

Prayer:

Thank You that even in my darkest moments You didn't leave. Even when I wanted to You to leave. Even when I said I don't believe. Even when my heart was hard and my mind was far from You. You waited patiently. You never had a bad thought towards me. You continued to believe the best in me. You saw my heart and You knew I was hurting. Even though I didn't know it.

Your graciousness and kindness to me is confusing. How could You stay when I wanted You to go? How could You love when I didn't care? I don't understand it and yet I'm eternally grateful. You are patient and kind.

May I accept Your love with gladness. May I give it to others with generosity. I have been given so much. Give me the power to understand how wide, how long, how high, and how deep Your love is so I may be made complete with all the fullness of life and power that comes from You. Amen.

Scripture:

And may you have the power to understand, as all God's people should, how wide, how long, how high, and how deep his love is. May you experience the love of Christ, though it is too great to understand fully. Then you will be made complete with all the fullness of life and power that comes from God. Ephesians 3:18-19

Ask God right now what He would like to say to you today. Start writing.

Continuing Your Love Affair

My deepest hope is that now you have begun to experience God's love for you like never before. My wish is that you continue on this journey everyday. Seeking first His kingdom and His love above all other earthly desires. It is then that He will grant you the desires of your heart.

Unlike most love affairs that come to a tragic end, this one can continue to blossom in the secret space of your heart. You can sneak away for a moment to reconnect. You can call and He'll always answer. God will never leave you. God. Will. Never. Leave.

God's love will not fail. He will continue to pursue you. You have the opportunity to respond and remove the blocks you've put up between you and Him.

It takes time to build a strong relationship. Start this 40-day love affair again. Let His love embrace you, his kindness overwhelm you, his gentleness speak to you. In stillness you will find Him…patiently waiting for you.

To offer your friends a free copy of The Ultimate Love Affair you can send them to the website www.ultimateaffairbook.com. All they have to do is cover shipping.

www.ingramcontent.com/pod-product-compliance
Lightning Source LLC
Chambersburg PA
CBHW050331120526
44592CB00014B/2138